Best Friends Forever

Friendship Quotes for You and Your Best Friend

TheQuoteWell

www.TheQuoteWell.com

Words are powerful! TheQuoteWell is committed to sharing inspiration and wisdom through the power of the written word. Visit our website for:

- Free quote collections
- Free tweetable images of inspiration
- Articles about Love, Life, Leadership, and more!

To: _Noelle_

From: _Cathy_

"We'll be friends forever, won't we, Pooh?" asked Piglet. "Even longer," Pooh answered. —A.A. Milne

Table of Contents

Foreword

This book is the result of many hours of research. Thousands of quotes were evaluated based on their relevance to the title, their ability to inspire, and for the accuracy of their citations. Unfortunately, curating quotes is an imprecise science. Great words are often borrowed. In some cases, multiple attributions can be found. In other cases, no attribution can be given. There are also many quotes that reflect similar sentiments worded differently. In the end, it is the burden of the editor to determine which quotes are used and who receives credit. Any and all content decisions made in editing these quotes have been in service of the deeper purpose of this book; to provide humor, wisdom, and perspective to the reader.

-Darren Weaver, Contributing Editor

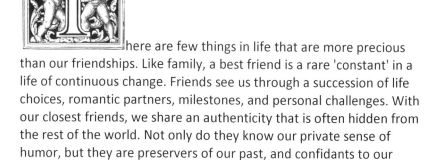here are few things in life that are more precious than our friendships. Like family, a best friend is a rare 'constant' in a life of continuous change. Friends see us through a succession of life choices, romantic partners, milestones, and personal challenges. With our closest friends, we share an authenticity that is often hidden from the rest of the world. Not only do they know our private sense of humor, but they are preservers of our past, and confidants to our hopes, dream, insecurities and fears.

Best Friends Forever celebrates friendship through a collection of carefully chosen quotes, from a diverse group of personalities both past and present. Divided into four chapters, each section explores a different aspect of friendship:

1) What Friendship Means
2) Defining a True Friend
3) The Value of Friendship
4) Wisdom About Friendship

This book is a testament to the friends in our life that we cherish most. If you received it as a gift, that person is YOU! May it help you recall memories of all that you have celebrated and supported each other through.

Chapter 1

What Friendship Means

Friends are like walls; sometimes you lean on them, and sometimes it's good just knowing they are there.
—Author unknown

One measure of friendship consists not in the number of things friends can discuss, but in the number of things they need no longer mention. —Clifton Paul Fadiman

Friendship isn't a big thing; it's a million little things.
—Author unknown

Friendship is the perfection of love and superior to love. It is love purified, exalted, proved by experience and a consent of minds. —Samuel Richardson

Friendship is a serious affection, the most sublime of all affections, because it is founded on principle, and cemented by time. —Mary Wollstonecraft

The function of a friend is not to have a function.
—Detlef Cordes

Friendship is held to be the severest test of character.
—Charles Eastman

We are each the star of our own situation comedy, and, with luck, the screwball friend in somebody else's. —Robert Brault

Friendship is love with jewels on, but without either flowers or veil. —Augustus William Hare and Julius Charles Hare

Sometimes the measure of friendship isn't your ability to not harm but your capacity to forgive the things done to you and ask forgiveness for your own mistakes. —Randy K. Milholland

Constant use will not wear ragged the fabric of friendship. —Dorothy Parker

Let there be no purpose in friendship save the deepening of the spirit. —Khalil Gibran

One's friends are that part of the human race with which one can be human. —George Santayana

Friendships are the family we make, not the one we inherit.
— Multiple attributions

Friendship is love minus sex and plus reason. Love is friendship plus sex and minus reason. —Mason Cooley

The true beauty of friendship is that it is bottomless.
—Roger & Sally Horchow

Friendship is by its very nature freer of deceit than any other relationship we can know because it is the bond least affected by striving for power, physical pleasure, or material profit, most liberated from any oath of duty or of constancy.
—Francine Du Plessix Gray

I always felt that the great high privilege, relief and comfort of friendship was that one had to explain nothing.
—Katherine Mansfield

The friend who holds your hand and says the wrong thing is made of dearer stuff than the one who stays away.
—Barbara Kingsolver

What is Friendship? Something deep that the heart can spend and keep, wealth that greatens while we give, praise that heartens us to live. —Henry Van Dyke

In friendship, your heart is like a bell struck every time your friend is in trouble. —Henry Ward Beecher

Friendship needs no words. It is solitude delivered from the anguish of loneliness. —Dag Hammarskjold

Wishing to be friends is quick work, but friendship is a slow ripening fruit. —Aristotle

The strong bond of friendship is not always a balanced equation. Friendship is not always about giving and taking in equal shares. Instead, friendship is grounded in a feeling that you know exactly who will be there for you when you need something, no matter what or when. —Simon Sinek

Friendship is almost always the union of a part of one mind with the part of another. —George Santayana

Friendship is two-sided. It isn't a friend just because someone's doing something nice for you. That's a nice person. There's friendship when you do for each other. —John Wooden

Depth of friendship does not depend on length of acquaintance. —Rabindranath Tagore

A friend is the only person you will let into the house when you are turning out drawers. —Pam Brown

As iron sharpens iron, so a friend sharpens a friend.
—King Solomon

Friendship should be more than biting time can sever.
—T. S. Eliot

Friendship is always a sweet responsibility, never an opportunity. —Khalil Gibran

Friendship needs a certain parallelism of life, a community of thought, a rivalry of aim. —Henry Adams

Friendship is the shadow of the evening, which increases with the setting sun of life. —Jean de La Fontaine

Chapter 2
Defining a True Friend

Lots of people want to ride with you in the limo, but a friend is someone who will take the bus with you when the limo breaks down. —Oprah Winfrey

Friends can be said to "fall in like" with as profound a thud as romantic partners fall in love. —Letty Cottin Pogrebin

I think part of a best friend's job should be to immediately clear your computer history if you die. —Mackey Miller

When we honestly ask ourselves which person in our lives mean the most to us, we often find that it is those who, instead of giving advice, solutions, or cures, have chosen rather to share our pain and touch our wounds with a warm and tender hand. The friend who can be silent with us in a moment of despair or confusion, who can stay with us in an hour of grief and bereavement, who can tolerate not knowing, not curing, not healing and face with us the reality of our powerlessness, that is a friend who cares. —Henri Nouwen

Friends are those rare people who ask how you are and then wait for the answer. —Author unknown

People come in and out of our lives, and the true test of friendship is whether you can pick back up right where you left off the last time you saw each other. —Lisa See

A friend is somebody who adores you even though they know the things you're most ashamed of. —Jodie Foster

An acquaintance merely enjoys your company, a fair-weather companion flatters when all is well, a true friend has your best interests at heart and the pluck to tell you what you need to hear. —E.A. Bucchianeri

Think where man's glory most begins and ends, and say my glory was I had such friends. —William Butler Yeats

"Friends don't let friends keep calling their exes and hanging up. Seriously. You have to stop." Alec looked furious. "So you broke my brand new phone? Thanks a lot." Jace smiled serenely and lay back on the grass. "You're welcome."
—Cassandra Clare, *City of Heavenly Fire*

True friendship never questions what it costs you.
—Stephen Richards

It was a huge comfort to have a person who'd keep you honest with yourself and who also gave you safe harbor.
—Lauren Dane, *Taking Care of Business*

One who sends you caring thoughts, prayers and love every day is indeed one of God's greatest Blessings. —Tom Hackett

A true friend is someone who knows what you want before you ask for it. —Vinita Kinra

A good friend will help you to discover the potentials you haven't uncovered. —Israelmore Ayivor

A friend should be one in whose understanding and virtue we can equally confide, and whose opinion we can value at once for its justness and its sincerity. —Robert Hall

Caring for, but never trying to own, may be a further way to define friendship. —William Glasser

True friends will always push you towards the great possibilities of your future; false friends will always chain you to the mistakes in your past. —Seth Brown

The rule of friendship means there should be mutual sympathy between them, each supplying what the other lacks and trying to benefit the other, always using friendly and sincere words. —Marcus Tullius Cicero

It is one of the severest tests of friendship to tell your friend his faults. So to love a man that you cannot bear to see a stain upon him, and to speak painful truth through loving words, that is friendship. —Henry Ward Beecher

If we would build on a sure foundation in friendship, we must love friends for their sake rather than for our own. —Charlotte Brontë

A real friend is one who helps us to think our best thoughts, do our noblest deeds, and be our finest selves. —Elizabeth George

Friendship is also about liking a person for their failings, their weakness. It's also about mutual help, not about exploitation. —Paul Theroux

A friend knows the song in my heart and sings it to me when my memory fails. —Donna Roberts

A true friend never gets in your way unless you happen to be going down. —Arnold Glasow

Only your real friends will tell you when your face is dirty.
—Sicilian Proverb

You can always tell a real friend. When you've made a fool of yourself, he doesn't feel you've done a permanent job.
—Laurence J. Peter

A friend is the one who comes in when the whole world has gone out. —Grace Pulpit

The best kind of friend is the one you could sit on a porch with, never saying a word, and walk away feeling like that was the best conversation you've had. —Author unknown

I like friends who, when you tell them you need a moment alone, know enough not to stray too far. —Robert Brault

A good friend is a connection to life, a tie to the past, a road to the future, the key to sanity in a totally insane world.
—Lois Wyse

A friend can tell you things you don't want to tell yourself.
—Frances Ward Weller

A friend accepts us as we are yet helps us to become the greatest version of our self. —Author unknown

A loyal friend laughs at your jokes when they're not so good, and sympathizes with your problems when they're not so bad. —Arnold H. Glasgow

The essence of true friendship is to make allowance for another's little lapses. —David Storey

A friend is a person with whom I may be sincere. Before him I may think aloud. I am arrived at last in the presence of a man so real and equal, that I may drop even those undermost garments of dissimulation, courtesy, and second thought, which men never put off, and may deal with him with the simplicity and wholeness with which one chemical atom meets another. —Ralph Waldo Emerson

As a friend, you first give your understanding, then you try to understand. —Robert Brault

Friendship is being there when someone's feeling low and not being afraid to kick them. —Randy K. Milholland

There is nothing like the razor sharp tongue of a good friend to cut through the lies we tell ourselves. —Laura Moncur

When someone allows you to bear his burdens, you have found deep friendship. —Real Live Preacher

To like and dislike the same things, that is indeed true friendship. —Sallust

Your friends will know you better in the first minute you meet than your acquaintances will know you in a thousand years. —Richard Bach

Your friend is your needs answered. He is your field which you sow with love and reap with thanksgiving. And he is your board and your fireside. For you come to him with your hunger, and you seek him for peace. —Kahlil Gibran

Our most difficult task as a friend is to offer understanding when we don't understand. —Robert Brault

A friend is one who does not laugh when you are in a ridiculous position. —Arthur Helps

True friendship comes when silence between two people is comfortable. —Dave Tyson Gentry

It is the friends you can call up at 4 a.m. that matter. —Marlene Dietrich

A true friend reaches for your hand and touches your heart. —Heather Pryor

A friend is someone who knows all about you and still loves you.
—Elbert Hubbard

A true friend freely advises, justly assists, readily adventures, boldly takes all patiently, defends courageously, and continues a friend unchangeably. —William Penn

A true friend is someone who lets you have total freedom to be yourself, and especially to feel. Or, not feel. Whatever you happen to be feeling at the moment is fine with them. That's what real love amounts to; letting a person be what he really is. —Jim Morrison

Friends show their love in times of trouble, not in times of happiness. —Euripides

Silences make the real conversations between friends. Not the saying, but the never needing to say is what counts. —Margaret Lee Runbeck

A true friend is someone who is there for you when he'd rather be anywhere else. —Len Wein

Sometimes being a friend means mastering the art of timing. There is a time for silence. A time to let go and allow people to hurl themselves into their own destiny. And a time to prepare to pick up the pieces when it's all over. —Octavia Butler

My best friend is the one who brings out the best in me. —Henry Ford

Love is blind. Friendship closes its eyes. —Friedrich Nietzsche

Friends: they cherish one another's hopes. They are kind to one another's dreams. —Henry David Thoreau

A quarrel between friends, when made up, adds a new tie to friendship. —Saint Francis de Sales

A true friend is one who overlooks your failures and tolerates your success! —Doug Larson

Our friends interpret the world and ourselves to us, if we take them tenderly and truly. —Amos Bronson Alcott

False friendship, like the ivy, decays and ruins the walls it embraces, but true friendship gives new life and animation to the object it supports. —Richard Burton

Yes we are friends and I do like to pass the day with you in serious and inconsequential chatter. I wouldn't mind washing up beside you, dusting beside you, reading the back half of the paper while you read the front. We are friends and I would miss you, do miss you and think of you very often. I don't want to lose this happy space where I have found someone who is smart and easy and doesn't bother to check her diary when we arrange to meet. —Jeanette Winterson

Though I can make a friend in an hour, it will take a lifetime to cultivate a friendship. —Jeffrey Fry

It is one of the blessings of old friends that you can afford to be stupid with them. —Ralph Waldo Emerson

If a friend is in trouble, don't annoy him by asking if there is anything you can do. Think up something appropriate and do it. —Edgar Watson Howe

The most I can do for my friend is simply be his friend.
—Henry David Thoreau

But if the while I think on thee, dear friend, all losses are restored and sorrows end. —William Shakespeare

He wipes tears off my face and then snot. He uses his hands. He loves me that much. —Nina LaCour, *Hold Still*

The most beautiful discovery true friends make is that they can grow separately without growing apart. —Elisabeth Foley

The tender friendships one gives up, on parting, leave their bite on the heart, but also a curious feeling of a treasure somewhere buried. —Antoine de Saint-Exupéry

Summer friends will melt away like summer snows, but winter friends are friends forever. —George R.R. Martin

What do we ask of friendship except to be taken for what we pretend to be, and without having to pretend. —Robert Brault

We are the captains of our own ships sailing the sea of life, but in times of a stormy weather, you will discover true friends when they don't hesitate to be a lighthouse. —Dodinsky

It's not how many friends you can count, it's how many of those you can count on. —Anthony Liccione

There is magic in long-distance friendships. They let you relate to other human beings in a way that goes beyond being physically together and is often more profound. —Diana Cortes

There is one friend in the life of each of us who seems not a separate person, however dear and beloved, but an expansion, an interpretation, of one's self, the very meaning of one's soul. —Edith Wharton

If you're alone, I'll be your shadow. If you want to cry, I'll be your shoulder. If you want a hug, I'll be your pillow. If you need to be happy, I'll be your smile. But anytime you need a friend, I'll just be me. —Author unknown

True friendship can afford true knowledge. It does not depend on darkness and ignorance. —Henry David Thoreau

The meeting of two personalities is like the contact of two chemical substances: if there is any reaction, both are transformed. —Carl Jung

Choose a friend as thou dost a wife, "till Death separate you." —William Penn

In everyone's life, at some time, our inner fire goes out. It is then burst into flame by an encounter with another human being. We should all be thankful for those people who rekindle the inner spirit. —Albert Schweitzer

Some people go to priests, others to poetry, I, to my friends. —Virginia Woolf

The friend in my adversity I shall always cherish most. I can better trust those who helped to relieve the gloom of my dark hours than those who are so ready to enjoy with me the sunshine of my prosperity. —Ulysses S. Grant

Rare as is true love, true friendship is rarer.
—Jean de La Fontaine

Cherish the friend who tells you a harsh truth, wanting ten times more to tell you a loving lie. —Robert Brault

The sincere friends of this world are as ship lights in the stormiest of nights. —Giotto di Bondone

Things are never quite as scary when you've got a best friend.
—Bill Watterson

Friendship marks a life even more deeply than love. Love risks degenerating into obsession, friendship is never anything but sharing. —Elie Wiesel

Friendship without self-interest is one of the rare and beautiful things of life. —James F. Byrnes

Being sad with the right people is better than being happy with the wrong ones. —Philippos

A good friend will find time on his calendar, a great friend never checks. —Jeffrey Fry

A friend to kill time is a friend sublime. —Haruki Murakami

Never hold resentments for the person who tells you what you need to hear. Count them among your truest, most caring, and valuable friends. —Mike Norton

Straight between them ran the pathway. Never grew the grass upon it. —Henry Wadsworth Longfellow

The most wonderful people possess their own unique sense of humour, but someone truly special will share yours.
—Ranata Suzuki

To be able to see into a friend's dream is a dream in itself.
—Yasutaka Tsutsui

We had grown into one another somewhere along the way. We were officially a team. —Shannon A. Thompson

What is a friend? A single soul dwelling in two bodies.
—Aristotle

You and I will meet again, when we're least expecting it. One day in some far off place, I will recognize your face. I won't say goodbye my friend, for you and I will meet again. —Tom Petty

If you come at four in the afternoon, I'll begin to be happy by three. —Antoine de Saint-Exupéry

I think of you as a friend. I used to think "friend" was just another word... nothing more, nothing less. But when I met you, I realized what was important was the word's meaning.
—Masashi Kishimoto

In my friend, I find a second self. —Isabel Norton

You bring magic into the world my friend, and with your magic this world becomes a better place to live in. —Author unknown

"We'll be friends forever, won't we, Pooh?" asked Piglet. "Even longer," Pooh answered. — A.A. Milne

Chapter 3
The Value of Friendship

We're born alone, we live alone, we die alone. Only through our love and friendship can we create the illusion for the moment that we're not alone. —Orson Welles

Friendship is the source of the greatest pleasures, and without friends even the most agreeable pursuits become tedious. —Thomas Aquinas

The greatest sweetener of human life is friendship. To raise this to the highest pitch of enjoyment, is a secret which but few discover. —Joseph Addison

True happiness arises, in the first place, from the enjoyment of one's self, and in the next, from the friendship and conversation of a few select companions. —Joseph Addison

I keep my friends as misers do their treasure, because, of all the things granted us by wisdom, none is greater or better than friendship. —Pietro Aretino

A best friend is like a four leaf clover, hard to find, lucky to have. —Author unknown

When we make friends, then we change from being animals to being human. —Stephen Richards

Hell will be Heaven with Friends, Heaven will be Hell without them. —Aman Jassal

If you have nothing in life but a good friend, you're rich.
—Michelle Kwan

Friendship is unnecessary, like philosophy, like art. It has no survival value. Rather, it is one of those things that give value to survival. —C.S. Lewis

The antidote for fifty enemies is one friend. —Aristotle

A friend is one of the nicest things you can have, and one of the best things you can be. —Douglas Pagels

Don't walk behind me; I may not lead. Don't walk in front of me;
I may not follow. Just walk beside me and be my friend.
—Albert Camus

Friendship is the golden thread that ties the heart of all the
world. —John Evelyn

Sweet is the memory of distant friends! Like the mellow rays of
the departing sun, it falls tenderly, yet sadly, on the heart.
—Washington Irving

The most valuable gift you can receive is an honest friend.
—Stephen Richards

The bird a nest, the spider a web, man friendship.
—William Blake

But friendship is the breathing rose, with sweets in every fold.
—Oliver Wendell Holmes

Friendship is a sheltering tree. —Samuel Taylor Coleridge

Friendship is Love, without his wings. —Lord Byron

The ornament of a house is the friends who frequent it.
—Ralph Waldo Emerson

Friendship is certainly the finest balm for the pangs of disappointed love. —Jane Austen

Friendship makes prosperity more shining and lessens adversity by dividing and sharing it. —Cicero

Friendship has been called the sweetener of life. It is a compound made up of truth and kindness, prudence and piety. —John Thornton

The company of just and righteous men is better than wealth and a rich estate. —Euripides

Friendship, like the immortality of the soul, is too good to be believed. —Ralph Waldo Emerson

Of all the heavenly gifts that mortal men commend, what trusty treasure in the world can countervail a friend?
—Nicholas Grimoald

There is no more precious experience in life than friendship. And I am not forgetting love and marriage as I write this; the lovers, or the man and wife who are not friends are but weakly joined together. One enlarges his circle of friends through contact with many people. One who limits those contacts narrows the circle and frequently his own point of view as well. —Eleanor Roosevelt

Nothing but heaven itself is better than a friend who is really a friend. —Plautus

True friendship is like sound health; the value of it is seldom known until it is lost. —Charles Caleb Colton

Walking with a friend in the dark is better than walking alone in the light. —Helen Keller

A new friend is always a miracle, but at thirty-three years old, such a bird of paradise rising in the sagebrush was an avatar. One friend in a lifetime is much, two are many, three are hardly possible. —Henry Adams

When the world is so complicated, the simple gift of friendship is within all of our hands. —Maria Shriver

But oh! the blessing it is to have a friend to whom one can speak fearlessly on any subject, with whom one's deepest as well as one's most foolish thoughts come out simply and safely. Oh, the comfort, the inexpressible comfort of feeling safe with a person, having neither to weigh thoughts nor measure words, but pouring them all right out, just as they are, chaff and grain together, certain that a faithful hand will take and sift them, keep what is worth keeping, and then with the breath of kindness blow the rest away. —Dinah Maria Mulock Craik

I have friends in overalls whose friendship I would not swap for the favor of the kings of the world. —Thomas A. Edison

Greater love has no one than this, that he lay down his life for his friends. —John 15:13

A man's friendships are one of the best measures of his worth.
—Charles Darwin

Friendship at first sight, like love at first sight, is said to be the only truth. —Herman Melville

No man can see himself unless he borrows the eyes of a friend.
—Colin Higgins

Of what use the friendliest disposition even, if there are no hours given to friendship, if it is forever postponed to unimportant duties and relations? Friendship first, friendship last. —Henry David Thoreau

I've learned that all a person has in life is family and friends. If you lose those, you have nothing, so friends are to be treasured more than anything else in the world.
—Prehistoric Ice Man, *South Park*

Loyalty and friendship, which is to me the same, created all the wealth that I've ever thought I'd have. —Ernie Banks

A single rose can be my garden... a single friend, my world.
—Leo Buscaglia

Without friends no one would choose to live, though he had all other goods. —Aristotle

True happiness is of a retired nature, and an enemy to pomp and noise. It arises, in the first place, from the enjoyment of one's self, and in the next from the friendship and conversation of a few select companions. —Joseph Addison

It is a good thing to be rich, and it is a good thing to be strong, but it is a better thing to be loved by many friends. —Euripides

A man cannot be said to succeed in this life who does not satisfy one friend. —Henry David Thoreau

Let us be grateful to people who make us happy, they are the charming gardeners who make our souls blossom.
—Marcel Proust

Friendship improves happiness and abates misery, by the doubling of our joy and the dividing of our grief.
—Marcus Tullius Cicero

In the sweetness of friendship let there be laughter, and sharing of pleasures. For in the dew of little things the heart finds its morning and is refreshed. —Khalil Gibran

To ensure that the self doesn't shrink, to see that it holds on to its volume, memories have to be watered like potted flowers, and the watering calls for regular contact with the witnesses of the past; that is to say, with friends. —Milan Kundera

Chapter 4

Wisdom About Friendship

It is not so much our friends' help that helps us, as the confidence of their help. —Epicurus

Friendship is not something you learn in school. But if you haven't learned the meaning of friendship, you really haven't learned anything. —Muhammad Ali

Most of us don't need a psychiatric therapist as much as a friend to be silly with. —Robert Brault

If a man does not make new acquaintances as he advances through life, he will soon find himself alone. A man should keep his friendships in constant repair. —Samuel Johnson

Letters of friendship require no study. —George Washington

The best rule of friendship is to keep your heart a little softer than your head. —Author unknown

Each friend represents a world in us, a world possibly not born until they arrive. —Anaïs Nin

Hold a true friend with both your hands. —Nigerian proverb

Yes'm, old friends is always best, 'less you can catch a new one that's fit to make an old one out of. —Sarah Orne Jewett

Do not protect yourself by a fence, but rather by your friends.
—Czech Proverb

In prosperity, our friends know us. In adversity, we know our friends. —John Churton Collins

Get not your friends by bare compliments, but by giving them sensible tokens of your love. —Socrates

We secure our friends not by accepting favors but by doing them. —Thucydides

You always think you could have done more. That's why you need a friend; to tell you did all you could. —Robert Brault

Even the utmost goodwill and harmony and practical kindness are not sufficient for Friendship. For friends do not live in harmony merely, as some say, but in melody. We do not wish for friends to feed and clothe our bodies; neighbors are kind enough for that, but to do the like office to our spirits.
—Henry David Thoreau

Friendship is essential to intellectuals. You can date the evolving life of a mind, like the age of a tree, by the rings of friendship formed by the expanding central trunk. —Mary McCarthy

The firmest friendships have been formed in mutual adversity, as iron is most strongly united by the fiercest flame. —Charles Caleb Colton

Friends and good manners will carry you where money won't go. —Margaret Walker

When you choose your friends, don't be short-changed by choosing personality over character.
—W. Somerset Maugham

Laughter is not at all a bad beginning for a friendship, and it is far the best ending for one. —Oscar Wilde

There is a magnet in your heart that will attract true friends. That magnet is unselfishness, thinking of others first. When you learn to live for others, they will live for you.
—Paramahansa Yogananda

Be slow in choosing a friend, slower in changing.
—Benjamin Franklin

Girls will be your friends. They'll act like it anyway. But just remember, some come, some go. The ones that stay with you through everything, they're your true best friends. Don't let go of them. —Marilyn Monroe

The actual secret to success: be a better friend today than you were yesterday. —Richelle E. Goodrich

As we travel life's long road, we meet and make new friends.
And even though the friends may go, the friendship never ends.
—Kunal Badlani

The language of friendship is not words but meanings.
—Henry David Thoreau

Nobody sees a flower, really. It is so small, it takes time. We
haven't time, and to see takes time, like to have a friend takes
time. —Georgia O'Keeffe

Strangers are just friends waiting to happen. —Rod McKuen

A man's growth is seen in the successive choirs of his friends. —Ralph Waldo Emerson

Since there is nothing so well worth having as friends, never lose a chance to make them. —Francesco Guicciardini

There are no rules for friendship. It must be left to itself. We cannot force it any more than love. —William Hazlitt

It seems to me that trying to live without friends is like milking a bear to get cream for your morning coffee. It is a whole lot of trouble, and then not worth much after you get it.
—Zora Neale Hurston

The best time to make friends is before you need them.
—Ethel Barrymore

Acknowledgements

This book would not have been possible without the efforts of a hardworking team of researchers. Their discriminating sensibilities have made this a significant collection of inspiration. Let inspiration be the next idea virus!

If you enjoyed this book and think others might also, PLEASE leave a five star review on Amazon!

About TheQuoteWell

Words are powerful! And no words are more powerful than inspirational quotes. TheQuoteWell is passionate about spreading hope, joy, wisdom, and humor through the power of the written word. Follow us on Twitter, Facebook, YouTube, and Google+ for access to FREE wisdom daily.

TheQuoteWell books are curated collections. Each book is the result of careful selection for only the best quotes from past through present on the subjects of Love, Life, Leadership, and more! The result is a chorus of profound wisdom emanating from a fascinating diversity of speakers. If you enjoyed this volume, visit our website for other titles.

Check out other titles from TheQuoteWell.
Available in paperback and all digital formats.

Made in the USA
Charleston, SC
28 February 2015